1 Will the Re...

I Want to Be Thin

Twyla is a thirteen-year-old who has always dreamed of being a model. She is already 5'6" and very mature for her age. What bothers her, however, is that she always has had a difficult time with her weight. Although most people would not consider Twyla overweight, in Twyla's mind, she isn't as thin as she would like to be—thin enough to be the model she would like to be.

For some time now, Twyla has been on a diet of less than 1000 calories a day. To make matters worse, Twyla has begun to go to the bathroom whenever she eats, and once there she vomits, hoping that the food she has eaten will not take its caloric toll and add to her weight. Twyla shares her story:

"Lately my parents have been on my case a lot because I don't eat much anymore. I mean, I eat popcorn and fill up on junk like that, but whenever I feel full, I just get rid of it. You know what I'm talking about. It really isn't that hard to do.

"I'm just so fat. I mean, I compare myself to all the models I see in the teen magazines I get, and there's no way I'm like them. Compared to them I might as well be Ms. El Blimpo.

"I'm not worried that much yet. My friend told me the other day that she knew where she could get some diet pills that work really well. I also started to jog after school. I figure if I can wear enough sweat clothes and jog far enough, the pounds will continue to fall off.

"I know what you want to tell me. You want to say that none of this should be so important to me. And you want to tell me that a girl my age shouldn't worry so much how she looks. But let me tell you something. When I've worked this hard already for the career I want, there's no way anyone could convince me that what I am doing is wrong or that it will hurt me.

"You simply don't understand. After all, I just want to be thin. Is that so wrong? And when I look at myself in the mirror, all I see is this fat blob looking back at me."

THE FIRST COMMANDMENT
You shall have no other gods.

What is this?

Answer: We are to fear, love, and trust God above all things.
(Luther's Small Catechism [LSC], page 13)

☞ What is the medical term for Twyla's condition?
☞ If you were Twyla's friend, what, if anything, could you do to help?
☞ When do you think Twyla will realize that she has a problem?
☞ How could Twyla be guilty of violating the First Commandment?
☞ Think of an ending to this story. What possible alternatives could happen to Twyla?

Can We Be Like God?

The story of the fall of Adam and Eve is a story in which both the man and the woman are tempted by the serpent to become like God. Read the story of the fall in Genesis 3:1-15.

☛ What reason does the serpent give Eve for God not wanting her to eat from the tree in the middle of the garden?

☛ The serpent says that once they eat from the tree, their eyes will be opened. Once their eyes are opened, what will they know?

☛ What kind of emotions do the man and the woman experience after they eat from the tree in the middle of the garden? What is their punishment?

☛ In what ways do people try to be like God today?

I Don't Know What I'll Do Now

Tom is a twelve-year-old who once dreamed of becoming a major league ball player. All his life he lived next to Cal, a boy who came within an eyelash of living out Tom's dream.

A superb high school all-American, Cal was a major league prospect who pitched his high school to the state title. In fact, Cal was chosen in the first round of the baseball draft by the New York Yankees and was scheduled to report to their minor league class-A farm team.

Needless to say, Tom was elated. He imagined the chance to go to Yankee Stadium just to see Cal pitch. Two days before Cal was to report, however, he went to a party with some of his friends and died without warning. The preliminary autopsy showed that Cal died of a drug overdose. Tom was devastated. He shared this story:

"I couldn't believe it when I heard it. I mean, Cal is gone? Just yesterday he was kidding around with me and telling me that some day I'd come up against him at Yankee Stadium and he was going to strike me out on three pitches.

"I know what they're saying. They're saying that he used drugs and that he died from a drug overdose. Let me tell you, if Cal used drugs, I would have known it. I mean, he told me everything—almost everything, that is. And if it's true what they say, then it must have been like his first time, kind of like that basketball player who was drafted by the pros so many years ago.

"Why would Cal even want to mess around with that stuff? He had too much to live for! Why would he even want to go to a party like that? He wasn't stupid! He knew what drugs could do to a person.

"I'm so angry. I'm mad at Cal. I'm mad at myself for wanting to be like Cal. I trusted him. I wanted to be like him. I put my faith in him. Now all that is gone. Cal is gone, and I really don't know what to do now. It's not fair!"

☛ Tom said that he wanted to be like Cal. What difficulties can a person experience when he or she wants so much to be like another person?

☛ Some people have said that society does not allow its sports stars, movie stars, and rock stars to be human. Do you agree with that statement? If people saw that celebrities were human beings no different from anyone else, what difference would that make?

☛ It has been said that everyone needs a hero. Why do people need heroes?

☛ Has Tom violated the First Commandment? If so, how?

TEN COMMANDMENTS / SESSION 1

Will the Real God...?

In the survey that follows, circle *Agree* if you believe the person is worshiping a false god; circle *Disagree* if you do not believe it.

1. A person who mortgages his or her house because of his or her gambling debts. *Agree Disagree*
2. A teenager who has a part-time job after school. *Agree Disagree*
3. A teenager who no longer wants to be with other friends because of the needs or wishes of his or her girlfriend or boyfriend. *Agree Disagree*
4. A forty-year-old parent who works 60 hours a week and then brings work home on the weekends. *Agree Disagree*
5. A teenager who collects every recording that a certain music group has made and then starts to cut his or her hair similar to the members in the group. *Agree Disagree*
6. A parent who plays golf every Sunday while his or her family attends church. *Agree Disagree*
7. A person who drinks a case of beer only on the weekends. *Agree Disagree*
8. An eighty-year-old person who doesn't believe in banks and stashes hundreds of thousands of dollars in shoe boxes while living in apparent poverty. *Agree Disagree*
9. A fifty-year-old who hides liquor bottles throughout the house so he or she can drink without anyone knowing about it. *Agree Disagree*

God Claims You

In your baptism God claimed you as God's child. God established a relationship with you through the Son, Jesus Christ, and the power of the Holy Spirit. That relationship is a gift of God's grace, given to you because of God's love—love graciously given, not earned. The relationship that God has given you is not destructive, nor is it deceitful. Rather, it gives you life, and it adds life to your other relationships.

In trying to keep the Ten Commandments, we are responding to God's gracious acts of love for us. Make a list of ways you plan to keep the First Commandment.

> "Be still, and know that I am God!
> I am exalted among the nations,
> I am exalted in the earth."
> The LORD of hosts is with us;
> the God of Jacob is our refuge.
>
> Psalm 46:10-11

⭐ And the Name Is...

Rate It

Karen was a normal, active, and intelligent thirteen-year-old. She attended church regularly. She was very well liked at her school. And she was the oldest of three children, which sometimes made her feel as if she had to be the role model for her brother and sister, a role that she often did not want to play.

One day she came home from school with an invitation to a sleep over from a girl named Michelle. Although Karen knew Michelle, she was not a close friend. When Karen found out that all her friends would be there, she was more determined than ever to attend. The invitation read, "We will be going to a movie and then out for some pizza. We will bring the girls home around 8:00 A.M."

Karen was not optimistic about her chances for attending the party, however. She knew her mother, and she knew how overly protective she could be. In spite of her fears and questions, Karen decided to show the invitation to her mother anyway, hoping that this time would be different.

When Karen showed the invitation to her mother, the questions began, and unfortunately, her suspicions were confirmed. "Karen, I need to call Michelle's mother and find out more details about this sleep over. By the way, what is the movie rated that you are going to see?"

"Mom," Karen said, "I think it's rated R, but it could be PG-13."

"What!" Karen's mother exclaimed. "There is no way I will allow my daughter to attend an R-rated movie. After all, to be rated R means there is too much sex and violence in it."

"But Mother!" Karen cried.

"And besides," Karen's mother continued without even catching her breath, "the language in R-rated movies is language I will not tolerate in this house."

"Mother!" Karen continued. "If you came to my middle school and heard the language I hear every day, you would have to rate my middle school R too!"

"Karen, I realize that," her mother said. "My problem with people who use bad language is that it shows so little respect. It shows so little respect for their relationships! I don't like that, and I don't think my daughter has to see movies like that!"

"Mother!" Karen cried.

☛ If your parent(s) came to your school and heard your classmates' language, would it be rated R?

☛ Karen's mother says that bad language is a sign of a lack of respect for people. Do you agree? Why or why not?

☛ If Karen were your daughter, how would this conversation be different?

☛ What makes youth, or any person for that matter, use language that is considered bad?

☛ What are your own limits for language? Do you talk differently depending on who you are with or the situation?

THE SECOND COMMANDMENT

You shall not make wrongful use of the name of the Lord your God.

What is this?

Answer: We are to fear and love God, so that we do not curse, swear, practice magic, lie, or deceive using God's name, but instead use that very name in every time of need to call on, pray to, praise, and give thanks to God.

(Luther's Small Catechism [LSC], page 14)

Names Are Special!

The story of Moses meeting God in the burning bush (Exodus 3:13-15) is one story used in Scripture to tell us just how special names really are.

In the Old Testament, God's name was Yahweh, the one who causes to be. In the New Testament, God's Son was named Jesus, which means "savior" (Luke 1:30-33). Read the story of Moses and the burning bush in Exodus 3:13-15.

☛ What name did God use in the midst of the burning bush?

☛ What other relationships did God claim?

☛ Should the name God be classified as a noun or a verb? Why?

But I Want People to Like Me!

My name is Bill. I'm 14 years old, and I love sports. When it's fall, I play football. When it's winter, my main game is hoops—basketball. When it's summer, I just love baseball!

When I'm not playing baseball in the summer, I just hang around with the guys and shoot hoops. It's really a lot of fun. What makes it even more fun is that when we play, we do a lot of "trash talking," just like the pros, if you know what I mean. When we do that, we feel cool, just like we were playing for the big money like most of the stars we like.

I know, if my parents knew, if my teachers or my pastor knew, they'd be upset. I don't want to upset or disappoint anyone, especially my parents or my pastor, but hey, it really doesn't mean anything. I mean it's not like I killed anyone or I've stolen anything. And besides, I want people to like me. I think if I didn't talk trash, no one would like me, and everyone would think that I'm weird.

☛ Bill thinks talking trash is cool. Do you have to talk like your heroes to want to become like them?

☛ Bill also says that he does not want to disappoint his parents or his pastor. Should the possibility that a person might offend or disappoint another person be a good reason to quit talking trash?

☛ Bill claims talking trash is not as bad as stealing or killing someone. Do you agree? Do you think there is an order of sins that makes one sin greater than another?

☛ Bill says that he talks trash because he wants to be liked. What do you think would happen if Bill decided to quit talking trash?

TEN COMMANDMENTS/SESSION 2

Is It a Wrongful Use of God's Name?

Answer the following statements by circling *True* if you believe the statement is true and by circling *False* if you believe the statement is false.

It is a wrongful use of God's name when:
1. someone prays before shooting a free throw. *True False*
2. someone uses God's name to sell a product. *True False*
3. television evangelists say God wants you to send money to support their programs. *True False*
4. someone prays for healing. *True False*
5. someone says "gosh dang it" when he or she is angry. *True False*
6. someone places his or her hands on the Bible before taking the witness stand in a trial and swears to tell the truth. *True False*
7. someone uses a horoscope to plan his or her day. *True False*
8. someone uses a seance board at a party. *True False*
9. someone says, "I swear. I was there; it happened!" *True False*
10. someone uses curses and street language but does not use the name of God when speaking. *True False*
11. someone refuses to walk under ladders or step on cracks. *True False*
12. someone is afraid of Friday the 13th. *True False*
13. someone makes the sign of the cross before stepping into the batter's box. *True False*
14. a professional sports team prays the Lord's Prayer together before beginning a game. *True False*
15. a pastor says, "I'm convinced the Lord has a plan for your life." *True False*

Respect the Relationship

Your name is important to you. You want people to respect you; you also want people to respect your name. Practice saying your own or a friend's name in different ways (angrily, excitedly, urgently, as a put-down, welcoming). Does your sense of self-respect change with the way the tone of your name changes?

How we speak—what we say and how we say it—can be a real indication of the respect we have for people and things. Think of ways you would like to continue to show people that you not only respect God's name, but you respect the relationship that God has given you as a child of God.

ALL HAIL THE POWER OF JESUS' NAME

All hail the pow'r of Jesus' name!
Let angels prostrate fall;
Bring forth the royal diadem
And crown him Lord of all.

⭐ To Go or Not to Go

We're Playing on Sunday

Tim was a reserve goalie on his traveling hockey team. It was a very good team, so Tim was glad whenever he had the chance to play, which unfortunately was very little.

Tim's big chance came when the starting goalie, Jim, suddenly had surgery for a ruptured appendix. Jim was expected to be out of action for at least three months.

Tim felt sorry for Jim, but at the same time, he was excited about the prospects of playing. Tim was in intense competition for the starting spot with another friend of his, Rich, who also was a goalie. The way things were going, Tim felt he had a slight edge over Rich.

The last tournament before the district play-offs was approaching, which meant that there would be games on Sunday, something that Tim always dreaded because it usually meant that he and his parents struggled about what to do about church. Tim was in confirmation class. He needed to do his worship notes, and on this Sunday he also had agreed to be a reader of the weekly lessons.

When Tim came home that evening after practice, he announced that he thought the coach would start him the next game and then said, "The schedule for the tournament just came out, and because of our record, we don't have a game on Saturday, but we're playing on Sunday."

"Well, that's too bad," Tim's father said. "The team sure will miss you!"

"What?" Tim cried. "I have to be there! If I'm not there, Rich will start! Besides, I never get anything out of church anyway."

"Tim, you're already behind in your worship notes, and you signed up to read the lessons on Sunday. It's already Wednesday and it's not fair to get a substitute now."

"I also promised to be a member of the team, Dad."

"Your coach will understand. After all, hockey doesn't have to be your entire life, you know!"

"Dad, I'm not going to church! I don't want to go!"

👉 Create your own ending to the story and resolve the conflict between Tim and his dad.

👉 Tim made the statement "Besides, I never get anything out of church anyway." What do you think people should "get out of church"?

👉 Tim has made two commitments, one to church and one to the hockey team. Which commitment should have the highest priority?

"...we should add a prayer for our parents..., that God may grant them understanding and wisdom...otherwise the devil will reign..."

(LW 43, 204)

9

TEN COMMANDMENTS/SESSION 3

THE THIRD COMMANDMENT

Remember the sabbath day, and keep it holy.

What is this?

Answer: We are to fear and love God, so that we do not despise God's Word or preaching, but instead keep that Word holy and gladly hear and learn it.

(Luther's Small Catechism [LSC], page 15)

The Sabbath Was Made For…

The sabbath has always been an important day in the life of God's people. The stories of creation and how Jesus observed the sabbath emphasize the importance of the sabbath day.

Read the conclusion of the creation story in Genesis 2:1-3.

☛ On what day did God finish the work of creation?

☛ Why did God bless and hallow that day?

☛ What were people expected to do on the sabbath day?

Read how Jesus observed the sabbath in Luke 4:16-23; Luke 6:1-5; Mark 1:21-28; and Mark 2:23-28.

☛ What did Jesus do on the sabbath?

☛ What did Jesus mean when he said, "The sabbath was made for humankind, and not humankind for the sabbath" (Mark 2:27)?

☛ What dangers might there be in being too busy to take time to hear God's Word and worship God?

Anywhere Is Fine

It was the first Sunday after confirmation. For three years, Darla had struggled on Saturday mornings to get through her church's confirmation program. She memorized her Catechism. She read her Bible. She completed her worship notes. She even finished her service projects. For all intents and purposes, she was a perfect confirmation student.

Now on this first Sunday after confirmation, Darla had made up her mind that she was no longer going to church. She would not be seen there. Of course it would be different if it were a wedding or a funeral. When her mother woke her on that first Sunday, their conversation went like this:

"Darla, it's time for church! We're going in an hour! Get ready!" her mother said.

"Mom, I'm not going!" Darla replied.

"Why?" Darla's mother asked.

"Because, Mom, now that I'm confirmed, I figure I don't have to go! After all, it doesn't make any difference if I go to church. I can worship God anywhere. In fact, later Sharon and I were going to go on a walk. I can worship God as much in nature as I can in church, can't I?"

"Darla, last Sunday you made a promise in front of the congregation and us that what we did at your baptism was the right decision. In a sense, you said that you would continue to come to church, and you would continue to participate in the Word and Sacraments! Didn't that promise mean anything to you?"

"Mom, chill out! It's not as if I don't believe or anything. I just don't see how my faith depends on my being in church every Sunday. After all, I'm a pretty private person. My faith should be between God and me. It's no one's business but my own!"

"Darla, get ready right now! I'm giving you 20 minutes to get ready."

☛ How would you answer Darla, who said that it didn't matter where she worshiped God?

☛ What promise will you make at your Affirmation of Baptism? (Check *Lutheran Book of Worship [LBW]*, page 201.)

☛ How would you respond to Darla when she said, "I just don't see how my faith depends on my being in church every Sunday.... My faith should be between God and me. It's no one's business but my own"?

☛ If you were Darla's mother, what else would you say to her?

The Sabbath and Worship

Respond to the survey by circling the answers that most accurately reflect your feelings.

1. I believe people can worship God anywhere and they don't have to go to church. *Agree Disagree*
2. The best thing about going to church is that you get to see your friends. *Agree Disagree*
3. The part of the worship service that means the most to me is:
   a. the hymns.
   b. the liturgy.
   c. the sermon.
   d. the prayers.
   e. Holy Communion.
   f. nothing.
4. If I could change one thing about our worship, it would be:
   a. to make the hymns more entertaining.
   b. shorter sermons.
   c. to change the liturgy so that I could understand it.
   d. to allow youth more significant roles within the worship service.
5. Attending church regularly helps me remember that I am part of a significant faith community: Christ's church—past, present, and future. *Agree Disagree*
6. Attending church regularly helps me continue to know that God loves me and Jesus died for me. *Agree Disagree*
7. I believe that the purpose of worship is to entertain people. *Agree Disagree*

I Was Glad When They Said unto Me

The New Testament church moved the sabbath tradition from Saturday to Sunday, a change made to remember the resurrection of Jesus. *Sabbath* means "seventh day," and thus the change in tradition eventually meant that the Christian church no longer observed the sabbath, or no longer observed the "seventh day." The church did not stop honoring God's directive to set aside a day for rest and worship, however. Rather, the new practice evolved to combine the sabbath tradition of rest and worship with the celebration of Christ's resurrection. The day of the week they chose for this new tradition was the first day of the week, Sunday. It is for that reason that the church today recognizes Sunday as the day on which we honor both God and the new beginning God gave in Christ.

Develop your own personal covenant promising to yourself and God how you plan to make worship a more important part of your life.

Christ comes to save us, we are forgiven. Christ comes to raise us, we are God's own. We are victorious: from his tomb given Life bright and glorious, never alone.

4 Family Ties

THE FOURTH COMMANDMENT

Honor your father and your mother.

What is this?

Answer: We are to fear and love God, so that we neither despise nor anger our parents and others in authority, but instead honor, serve, obey, love, and respect them.
(Luther's Small Catechism [LSC], page 16)

Susie's New Bike

Susie Diggins was her parents' pride and joy. An energetic six-year-old, Susie had just learned to ride a bike by practicing every day on a neighbor's old bicycle.

Her parents wanted to reward her, so one day they went out and bought Susie a brand-new, shiny bike. Susie was ecstatic as she got off the school bus that day and saw her new bike resting on its kickstand in the driveway. She could hardly wait to ride it.

When Susie's dad came home, she and her dad went out to the bike and, strangely, her dad only said to her, "Susie, it's all yours! Ride it wherever you want to ride it. Ride it for as long as you want. I know you won't take any chances, so I won't tell you where to go or when I want you to be home. I know you'll have a great time."

Susie rode and rode. She rode her bike as fast as she could. She rode down the side streets, and then she turned on the busiest street in her neighborhood. Susie began to feel scared. She wasn't having a good time. She didn't know what to do.

Susie's parents began to worry when Susie did not return home for supper. Her mother said to Susie's father, "Paul, I think you'd better look for her. We should have been more strict and told her where we wanted her to go and when we wanted her to be home."

Paul Diggins drove throughout the neighborhood. He drove to Susie's school. He drove past their church. He drove to the neighborhood park where Susie loved to play. There was no sign of Susie anywhere.

Later that evening, a knock was heard on Susie's parents' front door. As Susie's mother opened the door, she was shocked to see a police officer standing there who said to her, "Mrs. Diggins, I'm afraid your daughter Susie has been injured in a serious accident. You and your husband need to come to the hospital with me immediately."

When Paul and his wife Celia reached the hospital, they found Susie in her hospital room and unable to do anything but talk very softly. Susie had broken both her legs and one of her arms. A car had hit her when she rode her bike through a stop sign.

When Susie saw her parents, she began to cry and said to them, "I'm sorry! I didn't mean to! I didn't know what to do! I didn't know where to go! I was so scared!"

Susie's parents just hugged her softly and said a prayer of thanks that Susie would be all right! Then they decided to make sure that they would never let an accident like that happen again!

👉 In what ways is this story realistic or unrealistic?
👉 If Susie were 16 instead of 6, how would the story change?
👉 Why do parents give rules to their children?
👉 What are some of the rules that your parents have given you? That you like? Dislike?
👉 Why did God give the Ten Commandments to the Children of Israel?

TEN COMMANDMENTS/SESSION 4

Who's in Charge?

The story of the lost son is a story of a young man's reaction to the difficulties of dealing with parental rules and parental concerns. Read the story in Luke 15:11-32

The younger son in the story left home because he believed he would be free from his father's rules and regulations. Did he find freedom?

☞ Do you believe there is ever a time when people are free from rules or expectations?

☞ When the younger son returned, the older son was jealous and implied that the father had not treated the sons fairly or equally. Do you agree?

☞ What causes brothers and sisters to be jealous of each other?

David's Dilemma

David's father was an alcoholic. Now that David was in junior high, he rarely invited friends over because he never knew in what condition they would find his father when they came to the house. When David's father was drunk, he was an embarrassment to David because of how he acted.

One day when David came home from school, his father gave him a bag full of empty liquor bottles and in his drunken state asked him, "David, your mother is on my case for drinking too much. Will you take this bag to the dumpster in the park and throw it there so your mother won't see the empty bottles?"

David just stood there and thought about what he should do next.

☞ If you were David, would you do what your father wanted?

☞ If David refuses, is he breaking the Fourth Commandment?

☞ What would be the most helpful thing for David to do?

☞ How can the Fourth Commandment help those youth who come from dysfunctional homes like David?

That's Amazing

For questions 1-3, mark where your opinion falls on the continuums. For multiple-choice questions, you may pick more than one answer.

1. **My parents are**

   lenient.   *strict.*

2. **My parents like**

   all my friends.   *none of my friends.*

3. **When I was born, I'm sure**

   I was the apple of my parents' eye.   *they needed to take an aspirin.*

TEN COMMANDMENTS/SESSION 4

4. When I grow old, the one sentence that will best summarize what my parents or stepparents said to me is:
   a. Do your best in everything you do.
   b. We love you and we are proud of you.
   c. We will always be there for you.
   d. I told you that would happen!
   e. Other _____ .

5. When my children grow old, the one sentence I want them to remember my saying to them would be:
   (You may choose one of the above, or make up your own.)
   _____ .

6. My parents' greatest fear is:
   a. that I will never leave home.
   b. that I will never find a job.
   c. that they will never be grandparents.
   d. that I might die before they die.
   e. Other _____ .

7. I can best honor my parents by:
   a. trying harder to understand their feelings.
   b. thinking about what I say before I say it.
   c. complaining less about how unfair life is.
   d. trying to be more responsible.
   e. I've had it! There's nothing I can do to honor my parents.

8. When I can't talk to my parents, the most significant adult I can talk to is:
   a. a grandparent.
   b. a teacher or pastor.
   c. an aunt or uncle.
   d. a family friend.
   e. Other _____ .
   f. There is no one I can talk to.

THE SERENITY PRAYER

God grant me the serenity to accept the things I cannot change, the courage to change the things I can, and the wisdom to know the difference. Amen.

God wants parents to give constant love and care to their children. Parents are human, however, and like all humans, they can fail to live and love as they ought. Whether or not your parents are there for you, though, God's grace for you remains constant. God continues to be your faithful parent. God provides you with an opportunity to talk with God and to know that God understands and cares about what is happening to you.

Worship Thoughts

The Serenity Prayer (see far left) can help you deal with the tensions that come in any family life. The prayer addresses what can be changed and what cannot be changed about a person. It is often easier to change your attitudes and perceptions about your parents than it is to change your parents.

Make a list of the attitudes and perceptions about your parents that you need to change. Then make a list of things about your parents that cannot be changed but that, with help, you can learn to deal with in a better way.

I can change

My parents won't change

⭐ 5 The Gift of Life

Isn't That Like Committing Murder?

My name is Erica. I am 12, and I live with my mom, Shirley, my dad, Erik, and my sister, Patti, who is 10. Oh yes, I almost forgot to mention my two brothers; Tom is eight, and Aaron is six.

It happened to my mom when she was attending my brother's kindergarten conference. My dad said Mom had this shooting pain in her head that wouldn't go away. She drove her car home and into the garage. She went upstairs, took two pain pills, and went to bed. When my dad came home from work, he found her in bed and he couldn't wake her up.

He called the ambulance and they took her to the hospital. Later, I was sitting in the waiting room when the doctor came up to us and said to my dad, "I'm afraid your wife has had a cerebral hemorrhage." That meant a blood vessel had broken in her brain. The bleeding caused Mom to drift into what the doctors call a coma. We could talk to her, but she couldn't say anything or move a muscle. They also put her on a machine called a respirator that did her breathing for her.

We waited for days, and we hoped she would get better. But each day it seemed to the doctors and to me that she was not going to get better. It was all so very scary.

Yesterday, the doctor came in to meet with all of us and said, "I'm afraid tests show that Shirley's brain is dead. She will never recover. I recommend that you consider discontinuing the respirator and letting her die in peace."

I couldn't believe it! It was like someone had hit me hard in the stomach. I couldn't catch my breath. I felt weak and dizzy all over. It seemed like I never would stop crying. I buried my face in Dad's shoulder and hung on.

That day when our pastor came to see us, I couldn't stand it any longer and I cried out, "Pastor, she's only 40 years old. If we pull her off the respirator, she will die! Isn't that like committing murder?"

The pastor didn't answer my question. All the pastor did was to pray this prayer, "O God, please guide and direct this family as they make decisions about life and death. As they do, let them know that your love for Shirley and for all of them never ends. For Jesus' sake. Amen."

I don't want my mom to die!

☛ If you were the pastor, how would you answer Erica's question?

☛ Do you agree with Erica that pulling her mother off the respirator would be like committing a murder?

☛ If you ever became unable to breathe without the help of a machine, or if you were in a deep coma with little or no chance of getting better, what decision would you want your relatives to make?

THE FIFTH COMMANDMENT
You shall not murder.

What is this?

Answer: We are to fear and love God, so that we neither endanger nor harm the lives of our neighbors, but instead help and support them in all of life's needs.
(Luther's Small Catechism [LSC], page 17)

15

TEN COMMANDMENTS/SESSION 5

Don't Get Mad—Get Even!!

The story of two brothers, Cain and Abel, the sons of Adam and Eve, is a story that deals with individuals who are mad enough at each other to get even. Cain was so mad, in fact, that he killed his brother Abel. Read the story of Cain and Abel in Genesis 4:1-16.

☞ Cain became angry when the Lord had no regard for his offering. What might Cain have done differently to express his anger in a more appropriate way?

☞ When the Lord asked Cain in verse 9, "Where is your brother Abel?" Cain responded by saying, "Am I my brother's keeper?" What do you think Cain was trying to say? How can we be our brothers', our sisters', or our neighbors' keepers?

"Were it not for this excellent commandment...the devil would instigate such a massacre among men that no one could live in safety for a single hour." (LW 43.205)

What's Wrong with Me?

My name is Rick. I'm 13 years old, and I just started a new school this year because my parents moved to a different town. I really hate it here. Each day at school I sit in front of this big strong kid in science class, and whenever the teacher isn't looking, he hits me in the back. Then he calls me names. He says to me if I tell my teacher, he for sure will find me after school and beat me up.

I really feel like I want to die. I hate my school, I hate him, and I hate myself. It's gotten so bad that I feel like I'm the person that everybody likes to make fun of. What bothers me is I don't know what I've done wrong. I don't know what's wrong with me.

Just because I don't like sports, and I don't listen to the same kind of music the other kids listen to, they think I'm weird. And because I've had a problem with severe asthma and really am not that strong, they think I'm a freak.

I miss my old town, my old school, and my old friends. Since I've moved here, I've felt like kids have been killing me piece by piece and inch by inch. If that's what they want to do, they could do it much better with a gun.

☞ Rick claims that the other kids have been killing him. Can we kill others by what we say and what we do?

☞ Do you know any Ricks at your school? What can you do to help them or treat them differently?

☞ Where can Rick find the power to change his situation?

TEN COMMANDMENTS / SESSION 5

It's a Matter of Life and Death!

1. If there were a war, I would serve and I would kill if I had to. *Agree Disagree*
2. I would kill someone:
   a. if someone were trying to kill me.
   b. if they were hurting or if they had hurt another member of my family.
   c. if they had killed someone in my family.
   d. Me? Never.
3. I believe that the death penalty:
   a. is wrong and should be abolished completely.
   b. should be expanded to include all crimes of passion, rage, or violence, including rape.
   c. only rids society of the alleged criminal but does nothing to prevent future similar crimes.
   d. should be determined by the individual states.
4. If I ever were in a comalike state and could not make decisions on my own, I would:
   a. want all attempts and all efforts focused to save my life, even if that meant that I was attached to machines indefinitely.
   b. want my parents, my spouse, or my children to make the decision they felt was best for me and my family.
   c. not want any life-support systems at all.
   d. The idea is even too scary for me to think about.
5. I believe that putting people down:
   a. is just part of life, especially for kids.
   b. is no different than killing, except you don't use weapons.
   c. comes from people who have low self-esteem.
   d. sometimes is justified, especially if they put you down.
   e. is done by people who have been constantly put down by others.

Life Is a Gift

Life is a gift given to us by God. We are called by God to be faithful stewards of that life—our own and others'. What are some ways you can be a more faithful steward of the life of grace that God has given you?

The Prayer of St. Francis

Lord, make us instruments of Thy peace.
Where there is hatred, let us sow love;
where there is injury, pardon;
where there is discord, union;
where there is doubt, faith;
where there is despair, hope;
where there is darkness, light;
where there is sadness, joy.

Grant that we may not so much seek to be consoled as to console;
to be understood as to understand;
to be loved as to love.

For it is in giving that we receive;
it is in pardoning that we are pardoned;
and it is in dying that we are born to eternal life.

⭐ 6 It's about Love

THE SIXTH COMMANDMENT
You shall not commit adultery.

What is this?

Answer: We are to fear and love God, so that we lead pure and decent lives in word and deed, and each of us loves and honors his or her spouse.
(Luther's Small Catechism [LSC], page 18)

I Don't Want To!

Chuck is a fifteen-year-old sophomore who attends a local high school. He has been controversial because he has had the courage to speak up about his views on chastity and faithfulness in marriage and the place that sex should have within the bonds of marriage. This is Chuck's story:

"This year I came to a decision. It really wasn't that difficult to make. Some people say I'm too young to make it. Others say I will never be able to follow through on it, especially when I meet the right girl. I say, it's important that I make my stand now and that my age has nothing to do with what I have decided for myself as well as what I wish others would decide.

"You see, I've made a decision to remain chaste until I am married. That means that I do not intend to have sex with anyone until after I'm married.

"I think it goes like this. God gave us our bodies, and God gave us strong sexual feelings as well. Mind you, I don't think they're wrong at all. But I think the only way they should be acted upon is when two people are married.

"For me, sex is a sign of love and of commitment. I want my marriage to begin on a note of trust, and not have my partner worried that she can never trust me.

"What I expect from myself, I expect from the woman I plan to marry as well. I want to marry a woman who also has waited until marriage. I want to trust her too.

"I see my commitment to a chaste life as a wonderful gift that I am giving to my future wife. After all, when two people are married, shouldn't they want to give the best of themselves to one another? I also see my commitment as a way to continue to protect myself, as well as my future wife, from all the crazy things and diseases that happen in this world of ours today.

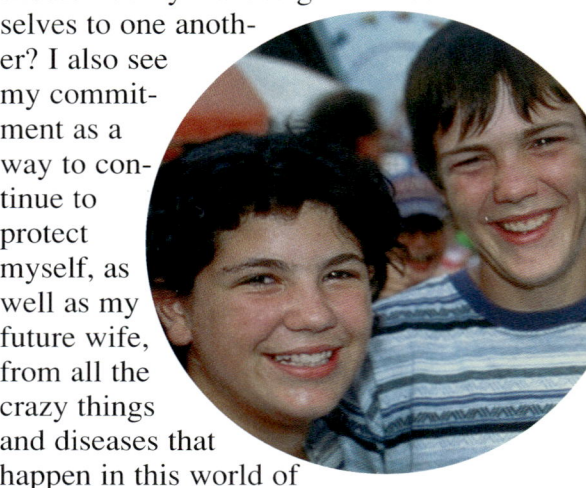

"I don't mind taking the stand I have taken, even if it means that a lot of times kids will make fun of me. I'm really glad that even sports stars are talking about the benefits of a position like mine. I sure hope we all do what we can to really turn sex back to what it was intended to be: to be used as a gift within marriage."

👉 How can remaining chaste be a gift to your future spouse?

👉 How can Chuck's position be helpful to those people who have made the opposite decision and yet wished they had not made that decision?

👉 Chuck expects that his bride-to-be also will have remained chaste until marriage. Explain why you think Chuck's expectation is either realistic or unrealistic.

👉 If you haven't made up your mind about this or other issues, what benefits are there in waiting until you're sure?

TEN COMMANDMENTS/SESSION 6

Called to Be Faithful

The story of Joseph and Potiphar's wife is a story in the Bible in which the main character, Joseph, struggles with the call to be faithful to God—especially as he deals with a member of the opposite sex. Read the story in Genesis 39:1-23.

☛ Of what crime was Joseph accused?

☛ What was the punishment Joseph was given?

☛ Have you ever been in a situation where you stood up for what was right and yet were punished because of it?

I Never Thought It Would Happen to Me!

Jenny Tolivor is 13 years old. She lives with her mom and dad and brother and sister. Jenny's mom and dad have been married for 16 years. The crisis in Jenny's life has just begun. One recent day after dinner, Jenny's mom told her and her brother and sister that she was divorcing Jenny's father. She said their father had found a girlfriend he would rather be with. This is Jenny's story:

"I never thought it would happen to me. I mean, I've had friends whose parents were divorced, but I always felt rather safe and secure. Sure, my mom and dad argued, but whose parents don't argue? It's all part of life, isn't it?

"When my mom told me that it had happened, I couldn't believe it. The first thing I thought was that Dad wanted to leave us because we kids never get along. I mean, we're constantly at each others' throats. I wonder if Dad just wanted some peace and quiet, and sometimes I think that if only we kids would have been a little bit more well behaved, none of this would have happened.

"But then, I should have seen it coming. For the last year or two, my dad has never been home. And then when he is home, he doesn't stay home very long. He usually just grabs a bite to eat and then goes back to the office. At least that's what he said.

"My trouble with all of this is that I'm not sure I can trust anyone anymore. Sure I love my father, but how can I trust him after he's left my mother for another woman? What's worse, I really wonder how all of this is going to affect me when it's time for me to get married. I mean, I see the pain my mom is going through. Since she's told us, it's like somebody died. She doesn't talk. She doesn't eat. And late at night I hear her rummaging around the house. I never want to go through what is happening to her.

"Maybe the best thing to do would be never to get married. I wish this never would have happened. I wish my father wouldn't leave."

☛ If Jenny came to you and said it was her fault her parents were divorcing, what would you say to convince her otherwise?

☛ Jenny says she will never trust anyone again. Would you feel the same way? Why?

☛ Jenny says that her parents' divorce might make her afraid of marriage and afraid of going through the pain her mother has experienced. What would you say to Jenny about the risks and the pain of marriage?

TEN COMMANDMENTS / SESSION 6

Marriage

What are some of your ideas about marriage? Circle **T** (true) or **F** (false), depending on which answer most closely reflects your own opinion.

1. It is important for both the man and the woman to come from similar family backgrounds. **T F**
2. If I get married, it will not make a difference if the person I marry is less intelligent than I am. **T F**
3. If I get married, it will not make a difference if my spouse earns more money than I do. **T F**
4. If I get married, the most important aspect about my spouse will be his or her responsibility. **T F**
5. I believe the church should make it more difficult for people to get married. **T F**
6. The decision to become sexually active affects only the two people who decide. **T F**
7. Abstinence is the most effective method of birth control. **T F**
8. Adultery means that a relationship has been broken. **T F**
9. I believe the state should make it more difficult for two people to be divorced. **T F**
10. God does not forgive the sin of adultery. **T F**
11. God remains faithful to us even when we are not faithful to God. **T F**
12. I believe that the media, music, and television:
    a. greatly encourage young people to be sexually active. **T F**
    b. have no influence in forming a young person's expectations for marriage. **T F**
    c. never emphasize the faithfulness or fidelity of marriage. **T F**
    d. always make relationships outside of marriage appear more attractive than marriage itself. **T F**

The good news in all the struggles that we encounter about sexuality and love is that God remains faithful to us, the people of God.

God's faithfulness and grace are new to us each day. It is that grace that can support us when we are confused about what's right or wrong. Answers aren't always easy or quick to come. But God gives us prayer, Scripture, and Christian community to help us at those times. What are some ways you and your friends can encourage each other to remain faithful in your relationships with God and with others?

I AM TRUSTING YOU, LORD JESUS

I am trusting you to guide me;
You alone shall lead,
Ev'ry day and hour supplying
All my need.

7 It's Mine and You Can't Have It

Duty, Honor, Country

Michael's dream came true when he was accepted into the United States Military Academy. Since he was young he had wanted to become an army officer like his father and grandfather before him.

During Michael's first year, he quickly became friends with Jimmy. Together they were surviving the trying and difficult first year at West Point.

The crisis in Michael's life came when Jimmy came to him and said, "Mike, I have a copy of the physics test for tomorrow—and the answers! I can't tell you how I got it, but man, we really need something like this, don't we?"

The problem was that Jimmy had violated the honor code of West Point, which said that a cadet would not lie, cheat, or steal. It also said that cadets who observed violations were honor bound to report those violations to the honor board. Michael tells his story:

"Very few guys get to live out their childhood dream like I've been able to do. Only now I have to make a decision. You see, when I entered West Point, I took an oath to uphold the honor code that said that I would never cheat or steal; and if I observed anyone who did, it was my duty to report him or her to the honor board. If I did that, the person who was guilty would immediately be kicked out of West Point. If I failed to do that, it would mean that I was as guilty as the person who cheated or stole.

"Now I have to make a decision, and it seems like either way I lose. If I turn Jimmy in to the honor board because of an honors violation, I will lose my best friend here. If I fail to turn him in, and I get caught, I will have to leave.

"I just wish Jimmy would have come to me before he got his hands on the test. At least we could have talked about it. At least maybe I could have helped him with the problems in physics.

"Now I'm not sure I know what I'm going to do. I love it here. But one thing I always have tried to practice is loyalty to my friends. I hate the spot I'm in. I feel I'll lose either way."

☛ Jimmy not only stole, he intends to cheat. How does cheating violate the Seventh Commandment?

☛ Why do people cheat?

☛ Michael's choice is to either turn Jimmy in or lie if asked if he knew anything about the stolen test. Under what circumstances would you lie for your friends? Why do you think it is so important for West Point to enforce an honor code?

☛ If you were Michael, what would you do? Why?

TEN COMMANDMENTS/SESSION 7

THE SEVENTH COMMANDMENT
You shall not steal.

What is this?

Answer: We are to fear and love God, so that we nether take our neighbors' money or property nor use shoddy merchandise or crooked deals to obtain it for ourselves, but instead help them to improve and protect their property and income.
(Luther's Small Catechism [LSC], page 19)

The Big Payback!

The story of Zacchaeus tells of one man's response to God's law and love. Read the story in Luke 19:1-10.

☛ Zacchaeus was called a sinner by those in the crowd around Jesus. Why?

☛ What does Zacchaeus promise to do in answer to the grumblers' protests and in response to Jesus' acceptance of him?

☛ What's more important—punishment or restitution?

☛ How does Jesus respond to Zacchaeus? Why?

☛ How does the Seventh Commandment relate to this story?

Short Change—Long Change

It was a very ordinary summer day for Cyndi and Shelley. They saw a lot of each other because they were neighbors. It made it so much easier that they liked each other as well and were friends.

Shelley was sitting at Cyndi's house one day listening to the radio when Cyndi's mother came into the room and asked if they could pick up some things at the store while she finished some work at home. Cyndi's mother gave them a five-dollar bill, and they walked to the corner store.

They put the juice and the cookies on the check-out counter, and Cyndi gave the clerk the five-dollar bill. The clerk put the bill in the register and then gave Cyndi change for a ten-dollar bill. Cyndi started to say something to the clerk when Shelley interrupted and said, "Cyndi, if we're late, your mom will be angry. We've got to go now!"

When they got outside the store, Cyndi said, "Shelley, didn't you see that? The clerk gave me change for a ten, not a five. We've got to go back and return the extra money. It doesn't belong to us!"

Shelley replied, "Are you serious, Cyndi? It's not our fault that the clerk can't add. After all, at least we weren't shortchanged. In fact, you might say that we were given long change. That's not all that bad, now is it?"

Cyndi said, "I think it's terrible, Shelley. It isn't our money. And if we take it, it'll be just like we're stealing it. I'm going to go back right now and give it back."

"Cyndi," Shelley said, "you don't need to do that! That little amount of money won't make any difference to that large store chain anyway. Look at it this way—Christmas came early this year."

☛ If Cyndi and Shelley decide to keep the money, have they stolen it?

☛ Do you think Cyndi and Shelley should return the money?

☛ Give the story an ending that resolves the conflict between Cyndi and Shelley.

22

TEN COMMANDMENTS / SESSION 7

Dear Sam/antha,

I've been thinking a lot lately about what's happening in the world. Every time I hear the news or read the newspaper, I learn about more people who don't have enough food, warm clothes, or medicine. Or I read about what's happening to the environment, how irresponsible so many people and big corporations are, and how destructive that is. I live on a farm, and sometimes I wonder if we are using fertilizers that are harmful and if that's worth the extra crop. But if there's a shortage of food, don't we have to do all we can to grow more?

And then there's stuff—just stuff. When we go to town and I see the huge garbage trucks making their weekly rounds, I can't believe how much stuff is being thrown away. I know I'm guilty too. I've got lots more than I need, but I don't have any more than most of my friends, and everyone sort of expects you'll have all that stuff.

Frankly, most people seem to have plenty where I live, or at least enough. I'm pretty lucky, I know.

Maybe that's why stories about people in need or the environment bother me so much. I'm trying to figure out where I fit in, if I should do something to help, and if so, what.

Thanks for any help,
Feeling Guilty

- Should *Feeling Guilty* feel guilty? Why or why not?
- How does the Seventh Commandment fit into the problems about which *Feeling Guilty* is concerned?
- What actions would you suggest *Feeling Guilty* take?

It All Belongs to God!

Probably one of the first things you learned as a small child was that it wasn't right to take something that didn't belong to you. That's one part of the Seventh Commandment. There's more, though. Everything that we have has been given to us from the hands of our benevolent God. "Our property" is a gracious gift from God. Our responsibility is to protect our property as well as the property of our neighbors and leave that property in better condition than when it was given to us.

How are the story characters you read about acting responsibly or irresponsibly in the way they care for property? What are ways you act responsibly in caring for your own or others' property? What things could you do better?

The way we care for God's gifts is one way we thank God for those gifts. Another is to offer prayers of thanksgiving. Create and then pray your own prayer, listing those things for which you are thankful.

Dear God, I thank you that you have given me

_____

_____

_____

and everything I need. Amen.

⭐8 Did You Hear What Happened To...?

I Can't Believe They're Saying That

THE EIGHTH COMMANDMENT

You shall not bear false witness against your neighbor.

What is this?

Answer: We are to fear and love God, so that we do not tell lies about our neighbors, betray or slander them, or destroy their reputations. Instead we are to come to their defense, speak well of them, and interpret everything they do in the best possible light.

(Luther's Small Catechism [LSC], page 20)

Toni, Katie, and Susan were close friends who did everything together. They went to the same church. They often liked the same boys. They also loved playing the same sports and sometimes competed for the same positions on the same sports teams.

Katie and Susan were trying out for starting point guard on the ninth grade basketball team. As Susan was driving in for a lay-up, Katie stole the ball and went the other way. As Katie went up for the lay-up, Susan's legs became tangled with her legs. Katie went down hard, and as she did she screamed out in pain, "I think I broke my ankle!"

As Toni rushed up to Katie, Katie cried out, "Susan pushed me on purpose!" Now it is Susan who tells her story:

"I can't believe this is happening to me, to us. Toni and Katie and I have been so close since we were little kids, and now it's like we never knew each other at all. I can't believe they're saying those mean things about me. I never pushed her. It's not my fault she's out for six weeks.

"I mean, my coach never said that I pushed her. She said it was an accident. But now I wonder if even she still believes me. What really hurts is that I thought we trusted each other, that we would stand by each other, but now it seems like things will never be the same again. Even worse is that they've started to say other things about me, like I'm stuck up, conceited. They say that I always try to butter up the coach and other teachers. They tell people I'm not nice.

"What bothers me is how the other kids are reacting. Wow, you really find out who your friends are. I don't know if I should confront Katie and Toni or not, and if I did, would they just try to twist what I say and use it against me and tell more lies about me?

"I wish this whole thing had never happened. I wish I had never gone out for basketball. I wish I had never been friends with Katie and Toni. Really, I wish we could be friends again."

☙ Have Katie and Toni broken the Eighth Commandment?
☙ Why do you think Katie and Toni continued to spread their story?
☙ What do you think will happen if Susan meets with Katie and Toni?
☙ What would you say to them in either case? If someone were saying something that was not true about you, how would you react?

TEN COMMANDMENTS/SESSION 8

To Tell the Truth

The story of Jesus tempted in the wilderness by Satan is an example of how the truth is stretched or misrepresented. Read the story of Jesus being tempted by Satan in Matthew 4:1-11.

☛ Did Satan really possess the power to do what he promised Jesus?

☛ In verse 6, Satan quoted from Psalm 91:11-12. How accurately did Satan quote from Scripture?

☛ Often Satan has been called the father of lies. How does the temptation of Jesus show that to be true?

What's Said Here Stays Here!

Bob and Peter were not friends; in fact, they barely knew each other until they found themselves in the same support group at school. The group was for students who came from troubled families. Bob's father had died several years ago, and Bob's mother had experienced a difficult time holding the family together. She worked two different jobs yet made only enough money to barely survive.

Peter, though living in a home with a father, found that life wasn't all that wonderful. Peter's father drank a lot, and periodically Peter's father would come home, yell and scream, and hit his mother. Peter, in fact, was very afraid of his father and feared that one day he would strike him.

Peter, however, never talked about his dad very much, and when he did, he only spoke of his dad's tendency for verbal abuse, not physical abuse. One day after school as Peter and Bob were walking out of the building, Peter stopped and talked to Bob for some time. He admitted how violent his father could be, and he said that he feared for his own safety. He also made Bob promise not to tell anyone about it. When Bob said he should bring it up at group, Peter replied, "I will in my own time, in my own way."

Three weeks later when Peter still had not said anything in the group, Bob suddenly spoke up, "Peter, I really think you should say something about how afraid you are of your father because he hits your mom all the time."

Peter didn't say a word. All he did was get up from his chair and close the door on the way out.

☛ If you were Bob, would you have said anything in the group?

☛ If you were Peter, how would you have reacted?

☛ Could Bob have handled his concern for Peter differently?

☛ Why might Peter not want someone in authority to know what was happening at home?

☛ Under what circumstances could you justify keeping information to yourself about your friends, even if in doing so it would lead to the physical harm of your friend?

25

TEN COMMANDMENTS/SESSION 8

Who's Bearing False Witness?

Circle **T** (true) or **F** (false) depending on whether you agree or disagree that the situation is one in which someone is bearing false witness.

1. Television news programs that report the news in a very objective manner. **T F**
2. Television news programs that really don't care what they report as long as they are able to sell their advertising and increase ratings. **T F**
3. Television news programs that give the viewers the kind of news they want to view. **T F**
4. Television news programs that dig into a candidate's or other public figure's personal life, even if what they report is true. **T F**
5. Tabloid newspapers that create stories solely to entertain their readers. **T F**
6. Gossip columnists in reputable newspapers whose job it is to "dish the dirt." **T F**
7. News magazine programs that fake experiments to come up with answers that support their position. **T F**
8. News magazine programs that pay their sources to get a story. **T F**
9. Witnesses who tell only what the police want to hear. **T F**
10. Television programs that edit all the material out of an interview that does not support their argument or case. **T F**
11. People who are paid to be expert witnesses for either the prosecution or the defense in murder trials. **T F**
12. A person who asks a friend, "Did you have too much to drink the other night when I saw you trip in the middle of the street?" **T F**
13. A person who repeats a rumor he or she has heard and fails to check out whether that rumor is true. **T F**
14. A person who tattles on a friend because what his or her friend is doing will cause bodily harm to that friend. **T F**
15. An arrested criminal who tells on his or her friends because he or she knows this evidence will get him or her a lighter sentence. **T F**

Our Reputations Are Important

God wants us to remember that our reputations are important. God wants us to protect not only our own reputations, but the reputations of our friends and our neighbors as well. The more we do so, the more we will trust one another and live in peace and harmony with one another.

Think of five ways that will help to protect the reputations of your classmates, friends, and families.

1.

2.

3.

4.

5.

BLEST BE THE TIE THAT BINDS

Blest be the tie that binds
Our hearts in Christian love;
The unity of heart and mind
Is like to that above.

9 All I Ever Wanted

Good Things Come to Those Who Wait

It was Teri's thirteenth birthday. She had arrived. She was officially a teenager. She felt very mature as she got out of bed that morning and went downstairs. Teri's mom was waiting for her.

"Happy Birthday, Teri!" her mom exclaimed. "Do you want to open your present from Dad and me now, or do you want to wait until you get home from school?"

"Hi, Teri! Happy Birthday!" her dad said as he sat down at the breakfast table.

"No, Mom, I think I want to open it right now!"

For months now Teri had dropped hints to let her mom and dad know that what she really wanted for her birthday was a new boom box combined with a CD player. She was sick and tired of her old radio. The reception was terrible, and besides, it was more fun for her to go to her friends' houses and listen to CDs then it was for her to invite her friends over to her house.

As her mother and father brought the present in, she couldn't hide her disappointment. "There's no way that could be what I wanted," she thought to herself. "This probably will be the worst birthday I ever have had."

She felt the box. It had to be clothes. She knew it was clothes. She opened it, and she couldn't believe her eyes. Not only was it clothes, it was probably the ugliest pair of jeans and a blouse she had ever seen.

Teri said, "Thank you!" very sheepishly and then ran to her room crying.

Her father followed her and asked, "What's wrong, Teri?"

"Dad, if you don't know, I'm not going to tell you!" Teri said.

"Teri, I'm a little slow, but why don't you give me a try?" her dad smiled.

"Dad, it's just that I wanted a boom box and a CD player just like Tina's. I mean, didn't you hear me drop a hundred hints? I couldn't have been more obvious. Now my friends will really think I'm weird."

"Yes, Teri, your mother and I knew that's what you wanted. But the way our budget is now, we decided that it would be best to postpone that until Christmas or your next birthday."

"Dad!" Teri cried. "Next Christmas is eight months away! And my birthday is another year. What am I supposed to do in the meantime?"

"Well, Teri, you know good things come to those who wait!"

☛ If you were Teri, what would your reaction have been?

☛ What would you say to help another person Teri's age who was disappointed because she or he didn't get what she or he wanted?

27

TEN COMMANDMENTS/SESSION 9

THE NINTH COMMANDMENT

You shall not covet your neighbor's house.

What is this?

Answer: We are to fear and love God, so that we do not try to trick our neighbors out of their inheritance or property or try to get it for ourselves by claiming to have a legal right to it and the like, but instead be of help and service to them in keeping what is theirs.

(Luther's Small Catechism [LSC], page 21)

They Had It All

The story of the rich, young ruler is about a man who had it all, but he believed that having it all was not enough. Read Luke 18:18-25.

☛ What was it that the young ruler was seeking from Jesus?

☛ What had the young ruler tried to do?

☛ What did Jesus ask him to do?

☛ What do you think Jesus really meant by his reply?

But I Want It and Need It

Name brands were important to Sam. Although he was only 12, he had the best name brand athletic shoes. He had name brand jeans. He had name brand shorts. He even had name brand underwear. Name brands to Sam meant that there was quality as well as status attached to the product.

The day came, however, when Sam's father and mother got divorced. After the divorce, Sam discovered that money was now running very low. Sam's father had just gotten a different job, but Sam knew they were going to have to cut corners just to pay the necessary bills.

One day as Sam was riding his bike, a name brand model that was only three years old, he met Franklin, who had the latest model with all sorts of neat innovations and in a great new color. Well, that was enough for Sam. Sam was bound and determined that he had to get a bike just like Franklin's. The only problem was that Franklin's bike cost almost $300.

That night Sam calmly announced to his father that he needed a new bike like Franklin's. Patiently, Sam's father asked, "And how much money did Franklin's new bike cost?"

"Dad, it's under $300. It's a great deal! Casey saw the same model for $400 at another store not far from here!"

"I'm afraid it's completely out of the question. We don't have enough money for luxuries like that now that your mom and I are divorced."

"But, Dad, I need it!" Sam said.

"No you don't, Sam! You don't need it! You want it! You've confused your wants with your needs," Sam's father said.

☛ How might Sam be guilty of violating the Ninth and the Tenth Commandments?

☛ Sam's father said that he had confused his wants with his needs. What is the difference between what we want and what we need?

☛ Do name brands guarantee status and quality as Sam believed?

TEN COMMANDMENTS / SESSION 9

Now and Then

Someone once said that our needs are few, and our wants are many. Think about what you need now at your age and what you want now at your age. Then think about what you will need 10 years from now, and perhaps, what you will want 10 years from now. Complete the following statements:

My age now is _____.

The things I need now are

The things I want now are

My age in 10 years will be _____.

The things that I will need then are

The things that I will want then are

How different are your lists? What changes more in 10 years, your needs list or your wants list? In what ways might that change your perspective on which things are wants and which things are needs?

The Bikes Are Never Better

The problems with the things that we want is that they often control us, they do not last, and their newness wears off. That new bike often sits in the garage when we discover new forms of transportation. The clothes that are so important to us and are in style soon become out of style. Read Luke 12:22-31 and then offer a silent prayer thanking God for giving you what you need.

THE TENTH COMMANDMENT

You shall not covet your neighbor's wife, or male or female slave, or ox, or donkey, or anything that belongs to your neighbor.

What is this?

Answer: We are to fear and love God, so that we do not entice, force, or steal away from our neighbors their spouses, workers, or livestock, but instead urge them to stay and remain loyal to our neighbors.
(Luther's Small Catechism [LSC], page 21)

10 Because God Cares

What then does God say about all these commandments?

Answer: God says the following: "I the Lord your God am a jealous God, punishing children for the iniquity of parents, to the third and fourth generation of those who reject me, but showing steadfast love to the thousandth generation of those who love me and keep my commandments."

What is this?

Answer: God threatens to punish all who break these commandments. Therefore we are to fear his wrath and not disobey these commandments. However, God promises grace and every good thing to all those who keep these commandments. Therefore we are to love and trust him and gladly act according to his commands.
(Luther's Small Catechism [LSC], page 22)

I'm in Deep Trouble

Hi! My name is Darrell. I'm 14, and I'm in deep trouble. You see, it all started when my friend Tad was over at my house after school. My mom, dad, and older sister work, so we were home by ourselves.

The only trouble with that is that when there's nothing to do, we can get pretty bored. Last Tuesday was one of those days.

So while Tad and I were watching television, a rerun that we've seen a hundred times, Tad said to me, "Hey Darrell, how come you have two cars when your mom drives to work with your dad?"

"I don't know—for weekend stuff, I suppose."

"Darrell, have you ever started that car?"

"Yeah, a million times!" I said. I also lied. I had never started it in my life.

That's when the trouble really started. We found the keys, went out into the car, and started it. I made a mistake. When I put the car in gear, I shoved the shift lever into reverse. Then I stepped on the gas pedal. The car shot out of the driveway, and I backed into the path of an oncoming car.

Fortunately, nobody got hurt, but I'm in deep trouble. First of all, my dad said there's no way he's going to let me get my permit at age 15. I mean, I make a mistake and he goes ballistic on me. He claims it's because he loves me and cares for me that he's doing that, but he sure could show his love and care in a better way than that. I don't know if he'll ever simmer down. Then again, he says that if he didn't love me, he wouldn't be angry and ground me.

Second of all, I've got to go to court. I'm really scared about that. I don't know what the judge will do. I don't know if I'll be put on probation. I really don't know what is going to happen. All I know is I'm in deep trouble, and I'll never let being bored make me do stupid things again.

☛ If you were Darrell's parent, what punishment would you have given Darrell? How would your parent(s) have reacted if you had done what Darrell did?

☛ How can punishment be an act of love and care?

What Did Jesus Do?

The story of Peter, who denies that Jesus has to die, is an interesting story because of Jesus' reaction to Peter's response. Read the story of Peter in Matthew 16:21-23. When Jesus announces that he has to die, what is Peter's response?

☛ How does Jesus respond to Peter?

☛ After the incident, Peter continues to be Jesus' disciple. Why didn't Jesus let this incident get in the way of his relationship with Peter?

☛ Read Luther's conclusion to the Ten Commandments on the left. How does this story relate to that?

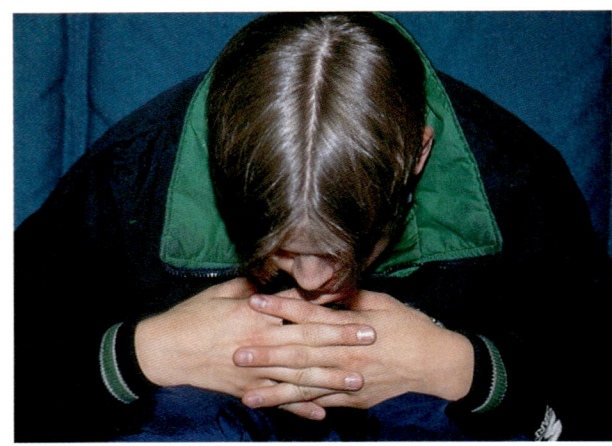